HOW TO USE THE THESAURUS

by Louise Colligan

SCHOLASTIC BOOK SERVICES
New York Toronto London Auckland Sydney Tokyo

ISBN: 0-590-11860-9

12 11 10 9 8 7 6   9/7 01 2/8

                                        11

Printed in the U.S.A.

CONTENTS

TO A THESAURUS

Franklin P. Adams

O precious codex, volume, tome,
   Book, writing, compilation, work,
Attend the while I pen a pome,
   A jest, a jape, a quip, a quirk.

For I would pen, engross, indite,
   Transcribe, set forth, compose, address,
Record, submit — yea, even write
   An ode, an elegy to bless —

To bless, set store by, celebrate,
   Approve, esteem, endow with soul,
Commend, acclaim, appreciate,
   Immortalize, laud, praise, extol.

Thy merit, goodness, value, worth,
   Expedience, utility —
O manna, honey, salt of earth,
   I sing, I chant, I worship thee!

How could I manage, live, exist,
   Obtain, produce, be real, prevail,
Be present in the flesh, subsist,
   Have place, become, breathe or inhale,

Without thy help, recruit, support,
   Opitulation, furtherance,
Assistance, rescue, aid, resort,
   Favor, sustention, and advance?

Alas! alack! and well-a-day!
   My case would then be dour and sad,
Likewise distressing, dismal, gray,
   Pathetic, mournful, dreary, bad.

Though I could keep this up all day,
   This lyric, elegiac song,
Meseems hath come the time to say
   Farewell! adieu! good-by! so long!

INTRODUCTION

What is a thesaurus? A medical dictionary of strange ailments? A rare South American tree? A prehistoric dinosaur? Or the Latin word for treasury? If you've ever used a thesaurus, you probably know this valuable reference book is really a treasury of words. With the aid of a thesaurus, you can replace worn-out words with lively, interesting ones.

You may be wondering, why own a thesaurus if you already have a dictionary? When you're looking for the meaning or pronunciation of a word, a dictionary *is* your best bet. But let's suppose you already know the meaning of a particular word that doesn't say quite what you want. A thesaurus gives you a choice of other words with similar meanings that better suit your needs.

Peter Roget, the English physician who organized the first thesaurus in 1852, thought writers needed a reference tool easier to use than a dictionary. He spent years grouping related words in categories, almost the way a botanist or zoologist might classify plants or animals. A true lover of words, Roget entitled his collection *Thesaurus of English Words and Phrases Classified and Arranged so as to Facilitate the Expression of Ideas and Assist in Literary Composition*. Modern adaptations of the thesaurus have shorter titles, but most publishers still honor Roget by including his name in their editions. Whether your thesaurus is a handy paperback or a thumb-indexed hardback book, its purpose is still to help you express ideas clearly, to assist you in literary composition.

So, with your thesaurus in hand, enjoy your treasure hunt for new, interesting words.

SAMPLE THESAURUS PAGES

Circled numbers explained on pages 10–13.

Category Thesaurus — Index Section

②
REGRESSION

④
REGRESSION, 283,287
REGRET 833, 950
regular *adjust* 23
  order 58
  arrange 60
rekindle *ignite* 384
  excite 824

①
INDEX

⑤
relieve *aid* 707
  comfort 834
relish *v. like* 394
  enjoy 827
remark *observe* 457
repair *mend* 658
  make good 660, 952

①
INDEX

resume *begin* 66
  repeat 104
revert *repeat* 104
  return 145
revive *refresh* 658
revoke *recant* 607
  cancel 756

②
ROSTER

riddle *secret* 533
  enigma 519
rig *dress* 225
  prepare 673
rim *edge* 231
romance *v.* 497
roster 86

8

Category Thesaurus — Main Category Section

③
478

478. DEMONSTRATION. — N. proof, evidence.
V. demonstrate, prove, establish, show.
Adj. demonstrative, conclusive, decisive.
479. CONFUTATION. — N. answer, disproof.
V. confute, refute, parry, negative.

⑨

③
484

483. UNDERESTIMATION. — N. undervaluation.
V. underrate, underestimate, undervalue.
Adj. pessimistic, unvalued.
484. BELIEF. — N. credence, trust, confidence.
V. credit, give faith, consider.

Dictionary Thesaurus

②
house

house, *n.* & *v.t.* — *n.* ABODE, residence, dwelling, habitation. *Colloq.* pad.
⑧

hum, *n.* & *v.i.* — *n.* buzz, murmur, drone. *v.i.* drone, murmur, sing. *Ant.* see LOUDNESS
⑥

②
hysterical

hut, *n.* shack, shanty, hovel. See ABODE
⑦
hysterical, *adj.* wild, emotional; frenzied.
See FEELING

9

WHAT YOU NEED TO KNOW
ABOUT THE THESAURUS

Many versions of Peter Roget's original thesaurus have been published since 1852. They are of two types: the dictionary thesaurus and the category thesaurus. This table shows how they are alike and how they differ.

	Dictionary Thesaurus	Category Thesaurus
Organization:	All the words you want to look up are arranged in alphabetical order as in a dictionary.	This thesaurus is divided into two sections. The front section contains related words grouped in numbered categories; the index section in the back lists words alphabetically.
How to Use:	Simply look up the word you want in the alphabetical listing.	1. Look up the word you want in the index. 2. Find the reference numbers for the categories related to your word.

3. Turn to the reference number in the main section. There, in the appropriate category, you will find your word along with many other related words.

Definition of Terms

① *Index:*	A dictionary thesaurus doesn't have an index.	Back section of a category thesaurus that lists words alphabetically.
② *Guide Words:* and ③ *Guide Numbers:*	Guide words are printed in bold type at the top right and left corners of each page in a dictionary thesaurus and in the index of a category thesaurus. All the words on the facing pages fall alphabetically between the guide words.	Guide numbers are printed in bold type at the top right and left corners of the main category section in the front of the thesaurus. All the categories on the facing pages fall numerically between the two guide numbers.

	Dictionary Thesaurus	Category Thesaurus
④ Entry Word:	The word you are looking up. Entry words are printed in bold type.	
⑤ Synonym:	A word that has a similar meaning to the entry word.	
⑥ Antonym:	A word that has nearly the opposite meaning of the entry word.	
⑦ Cross-Reference Word:	A word in small capital letters that tells you to see an entry word with a similar meaning.	A category thesaurus doesn't use cross-reference words.

⑧ *Slang,*
Colloquial,
Dialectal:

Nonstandard, informal, or regional uses of a word.

Abbreviations: *Coll.* or *Colloq.* = Colloquial
Dia. or *Dial.* = Dialectal

⑨ *Parts of*
Speech:

Parts of speech show how a word can be used
in a sentence. Abbreviations:

n.	= noun	*adv.*	= adverb
v.	= verb	*pron.*	= pronoun
v.i.	= intransitive verb	*prep.*	= preposition
v.t.	= transitive verb	*conj.*	= conjunction
adj.	= adjective	*interj.*	= interjection

EXERCISE A: **Matching Definitions**

Match the definitions in Column A with words in Column B by placing the correct number in the blanks provided. The first two examples are done for you.

Column A

Column B

1. __3__ A word that has a similar meaning to an entry word

1. Slang, colloquial, dialectal

2. __9__ Words on the top corner pages of a dictionary thesaurus

2. Guide numbers

3. _____ Nonstandard, informal, or regional uses of a word

3. Synonym

4. _____ Numbers on the top corner pages of a category thesaurus

4. Category thesaurus

5. _____ Thesaurus arranged only in alphabetical order

5. Entry words

6. _____ Different ways a word can be used in a sentence

6. Antonym

7. _____ A word that means nearly the opposite of an entry word

7. Dictionary thesaurus

8. _____ Thesaurus arranged in numbered categories of related words and ideas

8. Cross-reference word

9. _____ A word in small capital letters that directs you to see a related entry word

9. Guide words

10. _____ The words listed in the thesaurus

10. Parts of speech

Check your answers on page 43

ALPHABETIZING

If you've ever used a dictionary, a phone book, or a card catalog, you probably know the information in these sources is arranged in alphabetical order. That is, all the entries are listed from *a* to *z*, letter by letter. The dictionary thesaurus and the index of a category thesaurus both follow alphabetical order. To sharpen your alphabetizing skills, try the following activities.

EXERCISE B: Jumbled Jungle

In the blanks provided, arrange the list of animal words below in alphabetical order. The first two examples are done for you.

1. okapi   1. _____aardvark_____

2. lizard   2. _____antelope_____

3. platypus   3. _____

4. aardvark   4. _____

5. giraffe   5. _____

6. llama   6. _____

7. antelope   7. _____

8. zebra   8. _____

Check your answers on page 43.

EXERCISE C: **Scrambled Synonyms**

In the blanks following, arrange the verb synonyms in alphabetical order. The first example is done for you.

scurried
scampered
scattered
skidded
scrambled

1. The wildebeest _scampered_,
    _____, _____,
    _____, and _____over
    the plain.

pranced
gamboled
romped
bounded
cavorted

2. The antelope _____,
    _____, _____,
    _____, and _____
    through the air.

chewed
champed
gnawed
crunched

3. The giraffe _____,
    _____, _____, and
    _____ the leaves of the acacia
    tree.

shook
waddled
shimmied
wiggled
squirmed

4. The platypus _____,
    _____, _____,
    _____, and _____
    through the forest.

howled
neighed
bleated
squawked
bellowed

5. In the mountains, the llama
    _____, _____,
    _____, _____, and
    _____.

Check your answers on page 44.

GUIDE WORDS AND GUIDE NUMBERS

When you open a dictionary thesaurus, you will find words in bold letters on the top corner of each page. These are guide words, and they will help you find words quickly. The guide word on the left page tells the *first* entry word for that page. The guide word on the right page shows the *last* entry word on that page. Every entry word on these two pages is listed in alphabetical order between the guide words.

A category thesaurus uses guide words and guide numbers. In the index section, you will find a system of alphabetical guide words similar to those in a dictionary thesaurus. In the main category section, guide numbers are used instead of guide words. The left-page guide number lists the *first* category number for that page; the right-page guide number lists the *last* category number on that page. Any category numbers that fall between these guide numbers will be on these two pages.

EXERCISE D: Guide Word Hunt

Take out your thesaurus and look up the words listed in the entry word column opposite. They will fall between the two guide words at the top of two pages in a dictionary thesaurus or on two facing pages in the index section of a category thesaurus. Write the left-page guide word in the left column and the right-page guide word in the right column. The first two examples are done for you.

Left-page guide word	*Entry word*	*Right-page guide word*
1. ___publicity___	puppet	___purpose___
2. ___ocean___	ocean	___only___
3. _____	groan	_____
4. _____	pulse	_____
5. _____	salute	_____
6. _____	expanse	_____
7. _____	soar	_____
8. _____	interfere	_____
9. _____	silly	_____
10. _____	mock	_____

Note: Because different editions of the thesaurus list different guide words, you will have to check your particular answers with your teacher.

EXERCISE E: Guide Number Hunt

This exercise can only be done with a category thesaurus. If you have one, turn to the main category section. In the blanks below, write down the left-page guide number in the left column and the right-page guide number in the right column for each of the numbered category entries listed in the middle column. The first two examples are done for you.

Left-page guide number	Category entry	Right-page guide number
1. __10-14__	15. difference	__15-17__
2. __45-51__	52. completeness	__52-57__
3. _____	743. obedience	_____
4. _____	54. compose	_____
5. _____	367. plant	_____
6. _____	943. selfishness	_____
7. _____	540. teacher	_____
8. _____	23. agreement	_____
9. _____	66. beginning	_____
10. _____	467. evidence	_____

Note: Because each edition of the thesaurus lists different numbers on the page, you will have to check your particular answers with your teacher.

WORN-OUT WORDS

Certain words and expressions in our language have been so overused, they have lost their power to make a special impression. The thesaurus will help you find new substitutes for these worn-out words.

EXERCISE F: Word Exchange

In the blanks provided, write down as many specific synonyms as you can find in your thesaurus for the worn-out, overused words listed. The first two examples are done for you.

1. pleasant: blissful, genial, delectable, cozy,

                    inviting, alluring

2. pretty: comely, delicate, graceful,

                    personable, refined

3. cold:

4. smart:

5. soft:

6. white: _____

   _____

7. sad: _____

   _____

8. nice: _____

   _____

9. happy: _____

   _____

10. ugly: _____

    _____

Check your answers with your teacher.

EXERCISE G: **Sentence Switch**

Write a sentence using the worn-out words listed in Exercise F. Then write a new sentence, substituting the worn-out word with a substitute from the thesaurus. Note how the sentence changes when you swap a fresher word for an overused one. The first two examples are done for you.

1. A. ___We had a pleasant trip to California.___

   B. ___We had a blissful trip to California.___

2. A. ___She had a pretty way of saying things.___

   B. ___She had a refined way of saying things.___

3. A. _____

   B. _____

4. A. _____

   B. _____

5. A. _____

   B. _____

6. A. _____

   B. _____

7. A. _____

   B. _____

8. A. _____

   B. _____

9. A. _____

   B. _____

10. A. _____

    B. _____

Check over your sentences with your teacher or compare them with sentences your classmates wrote.

FINDING THE RIGHT WORD

Although synonyms are words that are alike, almost always there is a shade of difference between them. Sometimes the difference is in the meaning of the word itself, and sometimes the difference is due to the way the words are used in a sentence. For example, two synonyms for *cup* are *mug* and *chalice*. While you might order a *mug* of coffee in a restaurant, a waiter would probably be puzzled if you asked for a *chalice* of coffee. The following exercises will give you practice in finding the most precise synonym for a particular sentence.

EXERCISE H: Precision Practice

In each of the sentences below, underline the most appropriate synonym for the listed words. The first two examples are done for you.

dull   1. The blade of that knife is quite (<u>blunt</u>, dense, slow).

focus   2. Their baby always wants to be the (nucleus, middle, <u>center</u>) of attention.

nip   3. The gardener has to (nibble, snip, bite) the roses to make them bloom.

kick   4. They got a (gripe, punt, thrill) from riding the tramway.

promise   5. He gave me his (affidavit, covenant, word) he would be there.

corner	6. That company has a (nook, predicament, monopoly) on the paper market.
copied	7. The students (mimicked, forged, transcribed) the notes from the blackboard.
fair	8. The weather was (equitable, just, pleasant) on Saturday.
pass	9. She received a free (notch, gorge, ticket) to the performance.
sing	10. The pianist asked her to (warble, hum, yodel) the tune.

Check your answers on page 44.

EXERCISE I: **In Other Words**

Using your thesaurus, find the most appropriate synonym for the entry word listed before each sentence. The first two examples are done for you.

rare   1. I'll have my steak slightly __underdone__ .

talk   2. The professor gave a __lecture__ on economics.

common   3. It is a _____ belief that taxes are too high.

lift   4. _____ the box from the table.

leap   5. Look before you _____ .

launched   6. The boat will be _____ at the marina.

precise   7. The teacher's pronunciation is quite

           _____ .

hit   8. The producer expects the play to be

           a big _____ .

column   9. A _____ of troops entered the town at dawn.

pitch   10. The conductor gave the singers the

right _____ .

Check your answers with your teacher.

STRONG AND WEAK WORDS

Synonyms express different degrees of strength and weakness in their meanings. For example, have you ever noticed the many ways sports announcers describe defeat? Teams are not only *beaten*, but also *trounced, demolished, routed, overcome, foiled,* and *vanquished.* All these words mean almost the same thing, yet *trounced* and *demolished* are much stronger ways of expressing the idea of defeat. The exercises below will give you practice in finding synonyms with the exact degree of meaning you want.

EXERCISE J: Rate-a-Word

Rate the following pairs of words according to the strength and weakness of their meanings. Put a **1** next to the stronger word and a **2** next to the weaker word. The first two examples are done for you.

1. ___2___ hate = ___1___ detest

2. ___1___ famished = ___2___ hungry

3. _____ arid = _____ dry

4. _____ large = _____ gigantic

5. _____ rage = _____ anger

6. _____ scold = _____ berate

7. _____ vagrant = _____ wanderer

8. _____ anguish = _____ worry

9. _____ strong = _____ powerful

10. _____ frosty = _____ glacial

Check your answers on page 45.

EXERCISE K: **Strong Words**

Look up the following entry words in your thesaurus and find two synonyms that have *stronger* meanings than the entry word. Write them in the blanks provided. The first two examples are done for you.

1. yell   =   shriek   roar

2. full   =   glutted   gorged

3. forever   =   _____   _____

4. energetic   =   _____   _____

5. wet (adj.) =   _____   _____

6. suspicion   =   _____   _____

7. quarrel (noun) = _____   _____

8. struggle (verb) = _____ _____

9. pretend   =   _____   _____

10. harm (verb) =   _____   _____

Check your answers with your teacher.

EXERCISE L: **Weak Words**

Look up the following entry words in your thesaurus and find two synonyms that are *weaker* in meaning than the entry word. The first two examples are done for you.

1. torrid = <u>hot</u> <u>warm</u>

2. solitary = <u>alone</u> <u>single</u>

3. weep = _____ _____

4. laugh (verb) = _____ _____

5. ecstasy = _____ _____

6. savage = _____ _____

7. horde = _____ _____

8. pain (noun) = _____ _____

9. humble (adj.) = _____ _____

10. enigma = _____ _____

Check your answers with your teacher.

EXERCISE M: **Sentence Turnaround**

In the following sentences, write one strong synonym and one weak synonym for the entry words listed. Then compare how the tone of the sentence changes in each case. The first two examples are done for you.

pulled

1. He ___wrenched___ / ___tugged___ the
   STRONG   WEAK
   toy away from the baby.

puny

2. He has a(n) ___stunted___ / ___undersized___
      S   W
   physique.

lazy

3. Her mother says she is
   _____ / _____ about
      S   W
   cleaning her room.

firm

4. The governor has a(n) _____ /
             S
   _____ commitment to conservation.
      W

noise

5. As soon as the teacher left the room,
   there was a lot of _____ /
             S
   _____ .
      W

thin

6. After losing twenty pounds, she
   looked _____ / _____ .
        S   W

alarmed   7. He was _____ / _____

                      s   w

        by the news.

funny   8. The audience found the play quite

        _____ / _____ .

                s   w

ugly   9. The decorator had never seen such

        a(n) _____ / _____ room.

                     s   w

rain   10. Despite the _____ /

                              s

        _____, the reservoir remained

              w

        fairly dry.

Check your answers with your teacher.

EXERCISE N: Name That Proverb

The sentences following are really well-known proverbs in disguise. You can make the proverbs clear by substituting the underlined words with their synonyms listed in the thesaurus. These synonyms can be found under related root words, singular or plural forms, or different tenses of the underlined word. For example, you will find synonyms for "congregate" after the entry word "congregation," and "dissipation" after the entry "dissipate." The first two examples are done for you.

1. Don't <u>enumerate</u> your <u>poultry</u> before they <u>concoct</u>.

   <u>Don't count your chickens before they hatch.</u>

2. Fowl of a <u>plume</u> <u>congregate</u> together.

   <u>Birds of a feather flock together.</u>

3. April <u>sprinkles</u> <u>fetch</u> May <u>blossoms</u>.

   _____

4. A <u>buffoon</u> and his <u>currency</u> are soon <u>severed</u>.

   _____

5. Once <u>charred</u>, twice <u>bashful</u>.

   _____

35

6. Populations who <u>dwell</u> in <u>glazed</u> <u>abodes</u> shouldn't <u>fling</u> <u>minerals</u>.

_____

7. <u>Speed</u> <u>manufactures</u> <u>dissipation</u>.

_____

8. He who <u>remunerates</u> the <u>piper</u> may <u>summon</u> the <u>melody</u>.

_____

9. All is <u>impartial</u> in <u>affection</u> and <u>strife</u>.

_____

10. You can't <u>possess</u> your <u>pastry</u> and <u>devour</u> it too.

_____

Check your answers on page 45.

Variations:

With your teacher's permission, hold a race to see who can figure out all the proverbs first.

Think up some common maxims and proverbs of your own and see if you can disguise them with thesaurus synonyms. Then show them to your classmates and ask them to guess the proverb.

EXERCISE O: **Thesaurus Code Messages**

Imagine a group of spies has been captured by foreign enemies who only know a few simple words of English. One of the spies thinks up an escape plan he wants to share with his fellow prisoners. He has to write down the plan in words the enemy won't understand. Translate the following simple messages into "thesaurus code" by substituting the underlined words with more difficult thesaurus words. The first two examples are done for you.

1. When the lights darken, I am going to grab the enemy's gun while he sleeps.

   When the beams extinguish, I am going to seize the adversary's musket while he slumbers.

2. At morning, three of us will lock him in this room and sneak out through the window.

   At the ante meridian, three of us will secure him in this chamber and skulk out through the casement.

3. Once we are in the yard, we will split into two groups.

   _____

   _____

4. One group will crawl toward the tower and overcome the guard.

   _____

   _____

5. The second group will run toward the gate and wait
   for the first group.

   _____

   _____

6. After everyone meets, they will climb the wall and
   jump down.

   _____

   _____

7. Everyone is to hurry down the road until they reach
   the crossing.

   _____

   _____

8. Everyone will rejoin a group and elect a leader.

   _____

   _____

9. Each group will then <u>move</u> in a <u>different</u> <u>direction</u>.

_____

_____

10. Finally everyone will <u>gather</u> at the <u>border</u> at <u>dusk</u>.

_____

_____

Check your answers with your teacher; then share your code with your classmates. You might enjoy writing your own "thesaurus code" and asking your classmates to translate it.

EXERCISE P: **Misguided Menu**

An ordinary little coffee shop is losing a lot of business to a fancy new restaurant next door. Instead of changing the food, the owner decides to change the words on the menu instead. Look up the entry words "food" and "vegetable" in your thesaurus to find exotic or offbeat synonyms for the food words listed below. Write down these synonyms in the blanks provided.

Supper _____ Menu _____

"Our food _____ is brought to you

from our renowned kitchen _____

Beverage   _____

Relishes   _____

Soup   _____

Meat   _____

or

Stew   _____

Vegetables _____

Snack   _____

Check your answers with your teacher.

SYNONYM RELAY GAME

Number of players: One group leader

Two teams of three or more students per team

Materials needed: Individual copies of the thesaurus

Index cards or small sheets of paper

Rules of the game:

1. Each student selects an entry word from the thesaurus and writes it down on an index card or piece of paper.

2. Each student then writes down the first *three* synonyms of that word on three separate cards or sheets of paper.

3. Group leader collects all the entry word cards and places them in two separate piles at each end of a large desk or table in front of the class. Leader then collects and shuffles all the synonym cards and places each one face up on the desk or table.

4. Three members from each team line up in rows.

5. Group leader calls out a starting signal.

6. First member of each relay team goes to the table, picks-up an entry word card from the pile, then finds one matching synonym card for that word. Student then hands the cards to the second relay member, making sure the entry word is on top.

7. Second relay member finds another synonym and hands the cards to the third player who then finds the last matching synonym card for the entry word.

8. One team member quickly checks the entry word and the synonyms in the thesaurus to see if they match correctly. The first team to match all three synonyms to the entry word is the winner of that round and gets one point.

9. Begin the relay again with three new team members until all the entry cards are used up.

CHECK YOUR ANSWERS

EXERCISE A: Matching Definitions (page 14)

1. — 3
2. — 9
3. — 1
4. — 2
5. — 7
6. — 10
7. — 6
8. — 4
9. — 8
10. — 5

EXERCISE B: Jumbled Jungle (page 16)

1. aardvark
2. antelope
3. giraffe
4. lizard
5. llama
6. okapi
7. platypus
8. zebra

EXERCISE C: **Scrambled Synonyms (page 17)**

1. scampered, scattered, scrambled, scurried, skidded
2. bounded, cavorted, gamboled, pranced, romped
3. champed, chewed, crunched, gnawed
4. shimmied, shook, squirmed, waddled, wiggled
5. bellowed, bleated, howled, neighed, squawked

EXERCISE H: **Precision Practice (page 25)**

1. blunt
2. center
3. snip
4. thrill
5. word
6. monopoly
7. transcribed
8. pleasant
9. ticket
10. hum

EXERCISE J: **Rate-a-Word (page 29)**

1. 2 — 1
2. 1 — 2
3. 1 — 2
4. 2 — 1
5. 1 — 2
6. 2 — 1
7. 1 — 2
8. 1 — 2
9. 2 — 1
10. 2 — 1

EXERCISE N: **Name That Proverb (page 35)**

1. Don't <u>count</u> your <u>chickens</u> before they <u>hatch</u>.
2. <u>Birds</u> of a <u>feather</u> <u>flock</u> together.
3. April <u>showers</u> <u>bring</u> May <u>flowers</u>.
4. A <u>fool</u> and his <u>money</u> are soon <u>parted</u>.
5. Once <u>burned</u>, twice <u>shy</u>.
6. <u>People</u> who <u>live</u> in <u>glass</u> <u>houses</u> shouldn't <u>throw</u> <u>stones</u>.
7. <u>Haste</u> <u>makes</u> <u>waste</u>.
8. He who <u>pays</u> the piper may <u>call</u> the <u>tune</u>.
9. All is <u>fair</u> in <u>love</u> and <u>war</u>.
10. You can't <u>have</u> your <u>cake</u> and <u>eat</u> it too.

NOTES

NOTES

NOTES